PROSTITUTION, NOT ALWAYS A CHOICE

I0782684

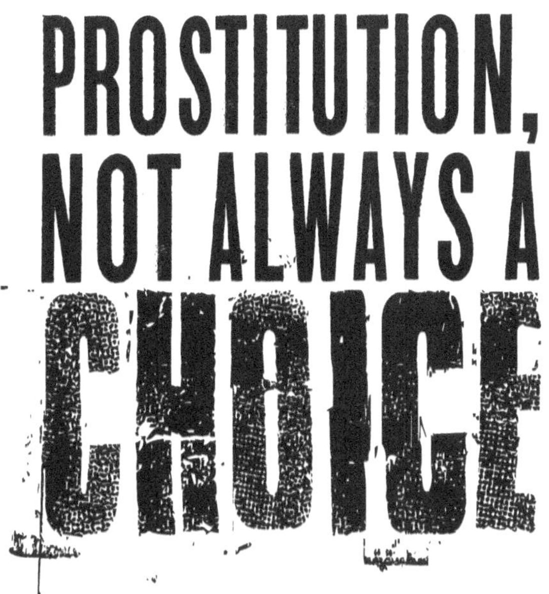

Mohd. Nasir Ali

Notion Press

Old No. 38, New No. 6
McNichols Road, Chetpet
Chennai - 600 031

First Published by Notion Press 2016
Copyright © Mohd. Nasir Ali 2016
All Rights Reserved.

ISBN 978-93-86073-77-8

This book has been published with all efforts taken to make the material error-free after the consent of the author. However, the author and the publisher do not assume and hereby disclaim any liability to any party for any loss, damage, or disruption caused by errors or omissions, whether such errors or omissions result from negligence, accident, or any other cause.

No part of this book may be used, reproduced in any manner whatsoever without written permission from the author, except in the case of brief quotations embodied in critical articles and reviews.

Life is like a game of chess, in which there are infinite numbers of complex moves possible.

The choice is open, but the move contains within itself all future moves.

One is free to choice, but what follows is the result of one's choice.

From the consequences of one's action, there is never escape

— Shelly Smith

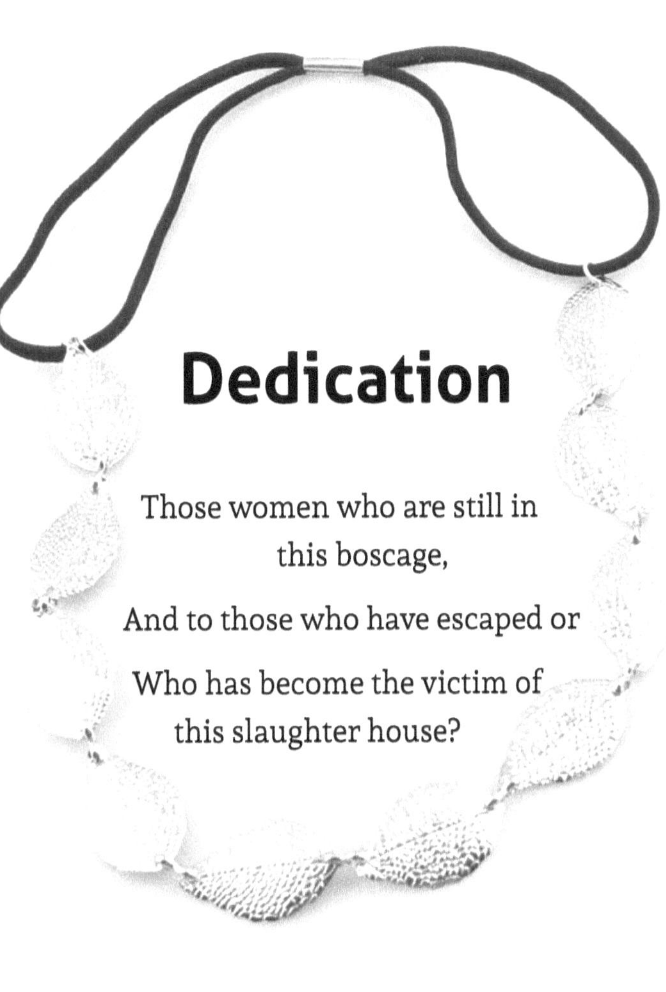

Dedication

Those women who are still in
this boscage,

And to those who have escaped or

Who has become the victim of
this slaughter house?

Contents

Acknowledgements   *xi*

Introduction   1

Orientation   3

Allahabad (Meerganj red light area story)   9

New Delhi (A visit to GB Road)   25

Mumbai (journey from Falkland Road to
Congress house)   47

Kolkata (a dark night in Sonagachi)   77

Reason for Entry   91

Conclusion   93

Acknowledgements

Thank you Almighty God for all the grace and blessings in my life. With the deepest gratitude I wish to thank every person who has come into my life and inspired and illuminated me through their presence.

I would also like to acknowledge and express my gratitude to the following people for their magnificent support and contribution to my journey and to the making of the book.

For sharing their story, love and divinity, I pay homage to Shagufta, Sweta, Nikita, and Anjali. (All names are changed to hide their identity)

Special thanks to Malini who told me or showed me the right path for my book.

For inspirational teachings and thoughts Dr. Ranjana Rajneesh, and Mr. Mandeep Yadav.

I would also like to thank my friends Zaheer Haider Khan (Ali), Aman Pandey, Prakhar, Kanchan, Richa, Naveen Chandra, Varsha, Shruti Mishra, Swati Singh and everyone else for their love and support.

A big thank you to the one who is always by my side and whose love and support known no limit. My courageous and beautiful mother Ms. Farzana Begum and my father Mr. Shamim Alam, my ideal, my strength, my love.

And a lots of love to my sister Tanveer and my late sister Nida Di whom I have never seen but believe that she was the best ever sister and the most beautiful girl on this earth.

And finally I would like to extend my gratitude to all my friends and family whose names I might not have mentioned here. Thank you all - from the bottom of my heart.

Introduction

A journey, which was started from the Allahabad red light area, then led me to Delhi's GB road, then to Mumbai's red light areas, concluded at last towards Kolkata. Throughout the whole journey, I met with lots of women and spent a night with them to hear their stories to come up with the truth, which we do not know about their real life. Through this book, one can imagine how these red light areas look.

"Prostitution Not Always a Choice" is all about the hidden truth of prostitution. The book conveys the message to the people that the women in this slavery really need help. They are not the garbage of our society. They want to escape this fate but no one thinks about this topic or to help them.

The story of four real girls has been related, who were forcefully pushed into this trade. The book also tells that women do not earn much money in this trade. They earn nothing and of the amount they earn, 75% of it goes to different brothel holders. It also tells that how painful it is to live a life, which we cannot even imagine.

It conveys a message that these women are not wrong; they are not a curse for our society. They are the only people who know and who face all this pain. They were also someone's sister, mother, daughter but poverty has made them do so. However, poverty is not only the reason, but also those corrupt people who just for their sake spoiled so many lives.

One rape leads to a lifetime of depression and women in this jungle get raped everyday twenty times, thirty times a day. Still no one is there to take a stand for them. The whole idea of paying for sex seems so undignified. Something so intimate in my opinion should not be up for sale.

Orientation

I was born into a middle-class Muslim family in Allahabad known for Sangam city in Uttar Pradesh, also known as "Prime Ministers city."

My father had not gone through for higher studies or much wealth; despite this disadvantage he possessed great innate wisdom and a true generosity of spirit. He had an ideal helpmate in my mother, Ms. Farzana Begum. She is a lady of simplicity and very hard working.

My parents were widely regarded as an ideal couple. We are two children, my sister and of course I, a tall and slim boy with rather average looks, born to tall and handsome parents. We lived in our ancestral house which was built during my grandfather's time. It was a small house made of limestone and bricks.

My grandfather used to avoid all things which were unnecessary and luxuries. Only the things which were necessary were provided in terms of food, medicines, or clothes. In fact, I would say mine was a very secure childhood, being taken care of by my mother. She has always wanted me to stay far away from anything which are of no use or are worthless for the future. She is like every mother who cares for her child but I must say, my mother is my best friend too.

Our locality was predominantly Muslim but there were quite a few Hindu families too, living amicably with their Muslim neighbors.

My father who is very hard working, with a down-to-earth personality, once told me " in his or her own time, in his or her own place, in what he really is and in the place he has reached good or bad every human being is a specific element within the whole of the manifest divine being. So why be afraid of difficulties, suffering and problems? When troubles come, try to understand the relevance of your sufferings. Adversity always presents opportunities for introspection."

These words of my father always helped me overcome the problems I faced writing this book or whenever problems or difficulties covered me.

During my journey to know about these women, I encountered a lot of difficulties and problems.

The very first problem was that the places I needed to visit were very new for me, and I was totally unaware of the environment of that particular area.

Facing the problem of a new place, I also needed to be aware of the local police of those areas because sometimes the police raid those areas.

Police being a barrier, I also needed to be aware of the brokers of those areas who charge you more than the real cost and are the barriers between me and my story.

One very big problem was finance. I usually get one thousand rupees as pocket money, but to complete my book I needed a handsome amount. Allah helped me out at every stage and showed me the path wherever I got stuck.

Among these problems, the biggest issue for me was to visit Meerganj (Allahabad's red light area) which was in my hometown. But my dedication towards my book and my motivation to convey the story of these women allowed me to leave behind all these problems.

I know I was lying to my father but I didn't want him to feel that his son cannot fulfill the dreams that every father has for his son.

My father has faith in me and this trust motivates me to prove myself to him... His inspirational words always teach me something. His advice to me was that, "Son, I know I have not studied a lot and I don't know what you are doing but I trust you. Whatever you will do, good or bad, you will do it yourself, and your future is in your own hands." I promise myself that I will always respect your words, Daddy.

Nobody wants to be a victim of violence, then what made these girls become sex workers? And what our government is doing to eliminate this flesh trade?

One fine night I decided to visit, read and talk to my friends about all the places where sex trade goes on. I knew that a righteous person would look at me with doubtful eyes and a decent person would never accompany me (no matter how many times they might have dipped their beaks and satisfied their balls), so I decided to do it alone and came up with the idea that I'll start with Meerganj (Allahabad) then GB Road (New Delhi), Kamathipura (Mumbai), and last but not least Sonagachi (Kolkata).

Covering the cities like Mumbai, Kolkata, the problem of funds was still there but I decided to deal with that later.

I wondered about the women who live in these places. What drives women into prostitution? Is it always by choice or are they forced into it? Why are they there? How do they look? How do they talk? Is it that those who are prostitutes are driven to do so because of their childhoods?

Before starting my journey, I was sure about one thing: that people from all strata of society- leaders of society, white color professions, almost people of every profession visit these red light areas to satisfy the uneasiness of their balls and do hanky-panky!

Allahabad (Meerganj red light area story)

Known as "Sangam city" is also known as "Prime Ministers city" that city has given seven Prime Ministers to India.

I was born here, in this beautiful city, surrounded by lots of historical monuments and religious places. But this beautiful city faces criticism for having a red light area since British rule. This is the place where sex workers were kept by the British for their entertainment.

Whenever I think of this city, the very first thing that comes to my mind is our first Prime Minister of India, Mr. Jawaharlal Nehru. He was a freedom fighter, a great orator and a well-read writer, to mention a few of his qualities.

Born to Motilal Nehru, Jawaharlal Nehru was born in Allahabad's Meerganj area. But little did anyone know that the place which gave birth to a great leader would one day turn into a hub of flesh trade.

"**Meerganj**," an area which is now full of those women whom we call them prostitutes, who share their bed with many people.

The area is situated in the city in a famous place which is known as "chock" where thousands of people go for shopping, mainly of the middle class. In this big market just ahead of Kothwali, there is a place covering an area of 10000/square ft. which is famously known as **Meerganj.**

Apart for local sex workers, many hail from the Indian states of West Bengal, Bihar, Jharkhand, Madhya Pradesh, and the neighboring countries of Nepal and Bangladesh. *These women are actively recruited by traffickers, pimps, brothel owners, organized crime members, and corrupt officials.*

During the visit, I saw many women on the street of Meerganj, waving to people pointing at them, making facial expressions to attract people passing nearby. The feeling was like I was passing through a fish market and the fisherman is calling me to buy his fish.

On the other side of the area I saw a police station; I guess it was just for the name's sake because I could hardly find any constables. I came across many young jaunty school boys who were dawdling around doing nothing.

The area is split into four lanes, every lane differs the age group. So I decided to see the whole area, therefore I started from the second lane, I saw the girls of seventeen – twenty-five years old calling people by attracting with their beauties. While walking, I saw that the lane (galli) is sub-divided into two parts; one takes you towards the police station side and the other one to the first lane entering point. I walked towards the direction which took me towards the first lane where I found women of many ages, fifteen to thirty-five years, some beautiful and some average and the lane was covered with pimps as well as with many men . On the starting point of the first lane you will find that a pan-wala selling his pan, cigarette, water, etc., a mittai-wala selling his sweets (I guess the sweets were not good to eat as they were all covered with flies). My God, such a big place. Large numbers of people were dawdling here and there as if this is the only place in Allahabad where women exist.

The area smelled so badly that it makes me wonder how these women even sleep in the room or stand to call for their customers.

After exploring the whole area, I felt tired and decided to sit somewhere. While I was resting, I was looking towards the environment, towards those women, their facial expressions, their smiles, their soreness, which was conveying many messages. I was trying to imagine a life of prostitute. Have we ever wondered about a prostitute's life? I believe no.

After resting for some time, I decided to approach a girl to whom I can talk to, to at least know something about this prostitution, about their life, how they feel and what they actually think about us. That is why I entered the first lane to find out a girl or lady who can at least share her hidden past with me.

Anyways, I was walking confidently in the lane but somehow there was a fear in me that I can be seen by someone I knew. While I was walking, I heard a voice of a man saying "Do you want a girl? I'll get a girl for you at a very cheap rate," it was my first encounter to such a situation, I ignored him and kept on moving but I was helpless to ignore the words he said to me.

Moving ahead, a lady called me, I guess she was thirty-five or forty years old. She looked like those same familiar faces I see every day, only, a little more tired with dark circles and wrinkles a bit more prominent. She said "You want pleasure, you sure you can?" with a smile, I replied. "Okay, how much do I need to pay you?" I asked as I found every person was asking the same thing. She said "rs 350" I said "okay."

I decided to go with her because she was thirty-five to forty years and I wanted someone who had been there for many years and she was the one I guess. Then she took me up the stairs where there was no light, and then I reached the first floor where I saw two rooms, one small one and one bathroom. Among them the first one was already occupied as it was locked and the voices coming from inside gave me the message that someone is there and suddenly I heard a voice from a lady, "Come on in, come inside the room."

I went inside the room which was stinking , there was a bed with very old bed sheet , a zero volt bulb for lighting lifeless poster of actor and actress and a very old fan which doesn't want me to give air .

She gave me the condom and started taking her clothes off, I said "Condom?" "I won't do without this," she replied. I was happy to know that at least they use this precaution and keep themselves away from life-taking diseases. "Okay, fine no need for this condom and no need to take your clothes off." She asked "Why?," I said "I am not here for sex or pleasure," she started laughing and suddenly she asked, "Are you impotent?," I looked at her and gave a smile and answered her, "No I am not." "Then what?"

Then I told her, "I am here to know about you people, your living standard, to know your past life. I want to tell the people that the things they know about you people is wrong. I am writing a book on you peoples to change the thoughts of the people towards you guys."

She was listening to me very carefully and suddenly she smiled at me and said "All over, now don't waste my time, if you want to do then do, otherwise leave the room," I said "Please" but she asked me to leave the room and I was left with no choice. I came out from the room and moved towards the stairs, but a moment I heard a voice saying, "Hey stop," I said "What?," she said "Come back to the room."

When I entered the room, I saw that she was looking at me very keenly. I looked at her too, and for once, I felt, I have never seen so much of truth in anyone's eyes before.

Then she asked me to sit and asked me to ask what I want to know. I said, "Everything, about you and about your past, how you entered here everything until date." Before she started, I took my pen and notebook out to write. She was lying on the bed and was looking at me very keenly and after a moment, I heard a sentence from her "I am a prostitute, working in the red light area of Allahabad. People look at us with disgust and scorn."

She asks me a question "Was I born a prostitute? NO. Even I was born in a respected family. Then why does society look at me as if I do not deserve to live?"

These words from her made me think to ask those people, why do they look at them so differently? Why doesn't deserve to live like other people in the society? I kept my pen and a notepad down and started listening to her.

She says "I was ten years old when my parents got me married to a man, much older than me. I was oblivious to the duties of a wife. I didn't know what sex was and my menstrual cycle had not started. I remember girls from my neighborhood going to school, how badly I wanted to be one of them! Marriage is supposed to be showered upon a woman like blessings, but to me it came like a shock. My husband forced me to have sex with him. He even had illicit relations with my sister in law.

"As the days passed, my objections were met with further torture. When I couldn't take anymore, I left his house and went back to my parents. When I was eleven, my mother started having physical relations with a man in my father's absence. Seeing my mother indulge in sex with another man, I was filled with curiosity and desire to experience it myself. There was a man in our locality that started coming to our house when I was alone. He forced me to do things for him.

"Since we were very poor, my father had to struggle to fill our needs and requirements. After sometime my mother came to know about that man but I don't know why she kept quiet. One day she came and asked me to go to the local contractor to have sex with him. "He will give us food to eat if you do certain favors for him," she said. I started going to him and he gave us atta, dal, and other eatables in return for sleeping with him. This carried on for a long time.

"When I entered at the age of twelve, my mother started bringing men to the house. When my father came to know about this incident, he beat me up and tried to strangle me. In a fit of anger, I left my house and went to my relative to search for a job.

"My aunt and uncle promised me a job in Allahabad as I trusted her and she brought me to Allahabad and sold me to a Nepali (brothel keeper) for rs 700. That moment changed my whole life and gave me the tag of "Prostitute."

"Since then it has been a roller coaster ride. I met a man who promised me a good life. I stayed with him for a few years after which he fell for a young girl and left me. Now, my life again came back to the same track to prostitution to support myself. During this time, my father died and I started supporting my family with my earnings. I got my brother and sister married. They are the same people who now don't allow me to enter their house because it affects their reputation.

"I remember that two men raped me once as they gave me a waitress job in a hotel and one day offered me a cold drink. I didn't know that he had mixed a drug in it and I became unconscious and was raped by him and his friend.

"Now I am forty years old. It has been thirty years of struggle to survive in world which does not respect women. That is my life story. I blame my mother for destroying my life when she cajoled me into this profession. A man suppresses a woman in our society. It is strange why a woman cannot understand another woman.

"All the women who work here have their own different or the same stories with one thing common: **no one has come here out of their own choice!**" And she stopped.

For the very first time I was listening to a woman who is locked in the brothel and that lady fostered respect in my heart. Women in this brothel, in their whole life, face so much of struggle and pain and we people says that these women are garbage "kachra" who are spreading dirt in our society. I want to know how they are spreading dirt in our society. A woman who is kidnapped or sold out at an early age in this jungle is forced to do this. Who wants to live like this?

While she was telling her story her face was saying many things. Even I could see that she wanted to cry but she didn't. She conveyed to me a message that even her tears have become so hard that they don't fall now. Each word she spoke felt as if I was being slapped hard. From that day, my idea of right and wrong changed forever.

To change her mood I said, "Oh hello, what happened, wait I'll get a cold drink for you and your favorite rasagulla," she smiled and said, "Don't mix anything in the cold drink." After having the drink, I asked to leave as it was getting very late for me. While I was leaving she said "Oh hero, tell me when is your book coming?" I said "Very soon," then she wished me all the best for my book and said that she'll pray that I get success for what I am and problems which comes in between. These words made a special place in my heart and then I took leave from there.

While walking on the street of the red light area, I was watching those women and during that time, one thing was disturbing me. That is the story of Shagufta is similar to these women or there is something worse.

The question asked by Shagufta that why does society treat her differently? Why doesn't she deserve to live? And was she born a prostitute? It made me wonder why it is so but I could find no answer.

I came back home and asked my mother to serve me dinner as I was very tired, or not exactly tired but very sad after hearing Shagufta's story. It was 11.30 pm, I was writing her story on my notepad. While I was writing, I asked myself why people don't see both sides before making any judgment, and what is the reason that people don't give respect and equality to them? Next day I woke up with many new hopes. While having breakfast I was reading the articles on internet about prostitution and I found one article related to the year 1988. The article says that there were 15000 prostitutes in the states and 12000 are estimated to be Nepalese. It talks about the Moolganj red light area that was in Kanpur where one lady, aged thirty-two, owns an establishment.

While reading this article one line of Shagufta strikes my mind that "a man suppresses a woman in our society. It is strange why a woman cannot understand another woman," seriously being a woman, why do they force women, why don't they help them? Strange but true.

I also found that in a day, an average Nepalese prostitute earns between rs 200 and rs 300, of which rs 30 goes as rent for a small room in which she handles her clients and rs 125 goes to the pool of didis and pimps whose responsibility it is to pay off the police. That leaves the girl with daily earnings of between rs 50 and rs 150.

It was shocking data for me that these women get such a little amount and the world thinks they earn a good amount. I was a little confused whether all the women in this brothel get the amount like this or some difference is there. To be sure of this I decided to find out in the other cities.

Days and days were passing and I was waiting for the month in which I supposed to leave for Ghaziabad as I was eager to know about everything, but I was unaware of the problems that were waiting for me in Ghaziabad.

September came and I started packing all my clothes and important things. On 16th of September I booked my train and on 15th, I went back to Meerganj to meet Shagufta. I parked my bike and started walking towards her. I went straight to her room but couldn't find her. I went down to look for her and suddenly I heard a voice saying "Oye idhar" I turned up and walked towards her. I found a smile on her face. I told her that I am leaving for Ghaziabad to study, and for my book too. She was looking happy and she told me to be aware of pimps and the policemen, and gave me the blessings for my book.

After meeting her I walked towards my bike and while walking I heard a voice calling "Oye... Oyee" I looked up and saw that she is calling me. I went back to her and asked her "what happened?" she said "Yaar... at least tell me your name na...?" I gave a smile and said "My name is Nasir," and then she asked for a hug and wished me the best of luck for my journey. An auspicious moment for me which I will never forget.

16 September was the day to leave Allahabad. I woke up a little late, had brunch and had a father and son talk. My father told me the dos and don'ts

that I need to follow in the new city as for the very first time I was going out of my city alone.

My parents came to depart me at the station. My father hugged me and my mother kissed me on my forehead and honored me with their blessings.

New Delhi (A visit to GB Road)

Ghaziabad was a totally different environment, porters asking me for taking my luggage, people pushing each other to get off from the train. I called one porter to take my luggage and help me to get off from the station. As I came out of the station, auto walas started calling me, so I hired one and ask him for Kavi Nagar. After the completely tiring day, I got everything settled.

Next morning with a lot of new information, I left for my institute. Weather was awesome. Birds were flying, and people were enjoying the weather. It was lunchtime; I found a tea stall nearby my institute. I went there and had tea and snacks as I was feeling very hungry.

This schedule continued for a long time and I had a good friendship with that tea stall person

Delhi GB Road. Number wise buildings where these women live.

Is it so easy to live a life in this jungle?

named "Praveen." We always had a good time during my lunch time.

One day I asked him about GB Road, he says "Ary kya zarurat Ann padi" I said "Bus aise e pucha bada naam suna hai dekh bhi liya jaye socha" then he told me the possible ways to reach there. I got everything and decided to visit the place in the coming Sunday.

It was a straight journey from Anand Vihar metro station to New Delhi metro station but in between, Rajiv Chowk was the station where I need to change to the yellow line to reach my destination.

Rajiv Chowk is a madly busy intersection where the metro's blue line meets the yellow line. Long queues had already formed on the station's platform by the time my train slowed to a halt. Through tinted windows, I could see a hundred pairs of eyes, wide open, wild with anticipation, staring back at the car. There was a brief moment of unsettling stillness. Then, "Ding" the doors slip open and I found myself stuck in the middle of the two powerful and opposing forces. From behind, an unstoppable mass of bodies barreled towards the exit and dispersed on the platform. To avoid succumbing to the surge, I jumped up and came out of the blue line metro and went down for the yellow line. Almost simultaneously, Delhi-ites of all ages dashed into the car like frenzied gazelles, scrambling here and there to snatch up the newly vacated seats.

I entered the yellow line facing the above situation. I couldn't do much but cling until the doors slid shut and all was calm again. Tranquility was restored and thirty uneventful seconds later, my journey was completed.

I was relieved to have control over my own body again. I came out of **New Delhi** metro station. I approached the cycle rickshaw stand on the street in front of the station. When I came out several of them had watched me emerge from the station and started calling to me after I accidently made eye contact with one of them. I asked him to take me to GB Road. He said "rs 15," and with a quick jerk of his head, motioned for me to take a seat.

We took off slow and steady, headed straight for the chaotic traffic of a major intersection.

So, let me tell you something about GB Road. GB Road also called Garston Bastion Road and has occupied many parts since the Mughal times when the sex trade extended across several sections of the city. Under British rule though, all the road light districts of Delhi were consolidated within a stretch of GB Road. Today around forty building 80 to 100 kothas (brothels) run and contain around about 12000 sex workers.

Every morning when the sun rises, one of South Asia's largest hardware markets awakens and thrives directly under the street's kothas. On the ground floor of the same buildings that facilitate the sex trade at night, you'll find shop after shop lining the sidewalks, specializing in all kinds of equipment. As the rickshaw wala plodded along, I leaned forward in my seat and tried to soak up the surroundings. I saw lifeless posters of Madhuri Dixit, Ajay Devgan, and Shahrukh Khan are plastered on the walls. When travelling down the left lane coming from the New Delhi station, all of GB Road's buildings are on the right. On the left, there is nothing but a wall that runs along the road as far as you can see. The raised divider somehow creates a significant sense of separation between the two sides of the road. Rickshaw wala left me nearby no 64 brothel and showed me where to go. I saw that kothas are located on the first and second floors of their respective buildings. Steep, poorly lit stair ways lead from the ground floor shops to the brothels above.

The kothas generally have a sitting room near the entrance where sex workers wait for clients. Many buildings also have balconies facing the main road where woman stand throughout the day and observe street goers observing them. Seriously, unless you make it a point to look up through, Delhi's largest red light district could very well pass unnoticed.

I walked towards the 64 no. brothel, after reaching I saw a board hanging on a wall and on that it was written **64 no kotha**, and just in front of that a cigarette and cold drink shop was placed where people were standing and smoking, and even if the girls want anything they could ask from there.

I entered the brothel, walked in a dark area of some 6 meters then suddenly I find women of age forty-five and above sitting on the left and right side and even in the centre on the way from where the stairs go to the first floor. Women were calling, pulling their customers towards them, abusing, eating paan, busy making up their faces to amp up their beauty to attract customers.

The area smelled very bad. While I was heading towards the first floor one lady pulled me towards herself and she held my shirt tightly I said "what happened, leave it" and I walked towards the first floor. When I was walking up the stairs I saw that on the first floor, the floor is divided into two parts, with the left side and right side full of girls' ages between sixteen to thirty-five years. Some were sitting, some were standing, some were attracting people with their beauty. The atmosphere was very hot, as comparing the total space with the crowd the place was very small as there was a large number of people. There was a counter where you usually give money when you go with the girl or if you want a cigarette or drinks you can get from there.

Religious scenery was hanging on wall. Girls with sleeveless saris, short dresses to attract people with their beauty. I was shocked to see the number of peoples visiting these places. The number of men, some sitting, some talking, some having chit chat, some just hanging around for entertainment. I do not get one thing: why do people come to GB Road for time pass? There are many more places in New Delhi to have a good time pass.

Is it because you are not charged to see these beautiful girls or are these women different to the women we see in our daily life? Or are they from a different planet?

The men who buy sex are exercising free choice, and it is this 'choice' to purchase vulnerable women and girls that expands prostitution and fuels trafficking for sexual exploitation.

I started looking for a lady or a girl to whom I can talk to know whether all the stories are same or different because many questions were running in my mind after visiting Allahabad's red light area. I saw a lady, I guess she was twenty-five or twenty-seven. I went to her to approach her as everyone did. She asked me to give rs 225 and I gave her. She went to a counter, took a token and told me to come with her.

She stood in front of a gate which was locked as I guess someone was already there. After five minutes or so, the gate opened. A girl came out of the room followed by a man of thirty to thirty-five years of age. The girl was abusing the man, I didn't know why.

After than she took my hand and pulled me into the room. It was a very small room with a bed, fan and a dim light. A few condoms were kept on the bed. She closed the door and jumped on the bed, started to undress herself, I said "No no- no need for this" she looked at me, I said "I am not here for fun, as I am looking for someone to whom I can talk and to know about them so I decided to start with you," she gave an awkward look and replied "No." A plea was on the tip of my tongue, but who knows how I came across for the wrong lady and after some time, she dressed herself and told me to go out from the room. I was left with no choice but to come out.

I do not know why she asked me to leave. What was the reason? I guess she was one of the women who hate us, who hate our society, our judgments. I even came across many women who replied, "See, one more helping man has come to know the story, tell him" and they started laughing. I do not know why.

I went out, had a cigarette and decided to visit again on the second floor. I believe I was not having a good time but for me to know about at least one woman was very important. I went to the second floor and on the left side of that floor I started looking but couldn't find one. I went on the right side too, but no result. While I was going to the ground floor, my eyes saw a lady wearing a yellow sari and a half sleeve blouse on the left block.

We had eye contact for a long time and without wasting my time, I went to her to approach for a full night to know everything. She got ready and I also asked her not to take any other person as I'll give her a good tip. I knew that this tip is very important for her because this is the only money which increases their income. She said "Okay." I told her that I'll come at night around about 9.30, but I guess she was not satisfied with my words so I asked her to get the slip for the whole night. After all this, I came out and went to find a good hotel to have dinner and I found one near the metro station.

While I was coming back towards 64 kotha, the whole atmosphere was changed. Shops were closed, women captured the area of the shop, pimps were getting the customers, and one of them approached me and asked me "You want girls?" I said "No, I stay nearby" and went back.

Oh man, a completely new atmosphere, with a police cab on rounds, was letting none of the people to stand on the lane. I went to the same brothel as I found the atmosphere not suitable. I directly went on the second floor to find Sweta but I didn't find her. I thought I got trapped again, but I satisfied myself and decided to look for her or to wait for her. I went to the first floor but why would she still be there? I came back on the second floor and was waiting for her, after sometime I relaxed because I saw the lady coming out from the room in the yellow sari. I found her sad, I don't know why? I asked her but she didn't reply. I asked to go to the room but she said "Wait, we'll go at eleven," I said "okay" and she sat down on the bench area just next to me.

I ask her again, "What happened, why are you sad?" She said, "Would you buy me a drink?" with no choice I said "Okay." She took the amount for the drink and got a beer for herself. She asked me what I wanted, but my religion did not allow me to drink. I said "No I don't drink." She looked towards me and laughed. I said "Hey, what happened?" but she says nothing.

I know why she laughed. She must be thinking that, my religion stops me from drinking, but does it allow me to come over here?

An hour passed and then she asked me to accompany her to the room. I followed her; she took me to one of the rooms which was just like the previous one. She sat down and said, "I want you to undress me," I said, "How can I?," she said, "Undress me because I'm tired" I looked at her and said, "No need for this yaar," she said, "What do you mean?," "I mean what you heard" I replied. She said, "Then why did you ask me for a full night?" I asked her, "Do you want to have more drink?" she was just looking at me and again she asked, "Why are you here? What do you want from me, as I don't have anything to give you?" I said "Okay, go and get a drink, then I'll tell you everything." She went to get a drink for herself and came up with two bottles. I said "Wow-wow lady you already had one!" but she said "Ary its all for the whole night, now tell me everything."

I told her about the previous incidents that happened to me and that I am here for my book that I am writing on prostitution to tell people about what they don't know about these women. I told her that I am here to know about her, about her past and I also requested her not to say to leave.

She said "if I say yes, then? I said, "Oh please," but she smiled and said, "In the very beginning I judged you. I've been here for a long time and I can easily judge people, and I know you are different from all these men who just come here for their pleasure, ask what you want to ask." Before she would have started telling her story she asked me a very funny question that, "Is everything fine na, I mean everything?" I laughed and said "Ya-ya don't worry," I knew what she was talking about. We were having a good time; she was sitting on the other side and me on the other. I asked her name, she told me "Sweta," and she hails from Orissa. Then I asked her, "How did you enter into this jungle?" She smiled and said, "Chill we are having a full night, let me tell you one story of a girl."

"This story is about a small girl who was known in the village for the sweet voice. Her father was a farmer and was having one brother and three sisters, all of them went to school. They were very poor.

"The girl was very beautiful as her voice was but one black day she met a boy to whom she wanted to marry, her songs changed to her love for him. The boy was older than she was as he was twenty-three. They started spending time together for hours. The boy told her tales of his far away travels to big cities, as she was impressed by everything about him- his bicycle, his radio, his goggles, and his clothes.

"After some month when she turned fourteen, he told her that he wanted to marry her. It is very common for girls to marry early in rural India. Since women are valued mostly homemaker and mothers, families have no incentive to keep their daughter in school.

"The older the girl gets, the more her family will have to pay for her dowry. Keeping all this in my mind she decided to run and marry. Her heart beat fast as they crossed Orissa in the darkness of night. She had never been to a big city like New Delhi and so she was distracted from the reality that she was leaving her family and her school.

"While she was in the train there was a terror of being caught, but thrilled at the prospect of settling down with the man whom she loved.

"Next morning, with very new hope of new life we arrived at the station. The boy told the girl that he wanted to keep her safe from his parents so he is taking her to her mammi's house. In a few days he would return for her. She was reluctant to see him go, but she trusted his decision. That night in the glow of moonlight, she saw girls in short shirts and red lipstick standing in a line on a street.

"The next morning she asked his mammi about those girls. She spoke to her in a hollow voice devoid of emotion. She was told that she had been sold to her by the man she loved, and now she would have to work by joining those girls each night.

"To break her in, she was

Raped several times a night

For nearly a month before the madam

Started selling her to men for money.

It was typical for her to have

Ten to twelve buyers every night."

"Her whole world was shattered into pieces. She has been tortured and abused, and survived serious injuries inflicted by buyer and pimps, but this pain was not big for her as the pain of being deceived by the man she loved.

"The owner of the brothel raped her, as he did to all new girls. He ordered the brothel madam to beat her with a leather belt every day. She was kept locked inside a room, with no food or water for days."

I stopped her in between and asked her "Whose story is this?" but she didn't stop and continued "They raped her several times a night for nearly a month before the madam started selling her to the buyers. They use to abuse her, treat her as if they owned her body. Even they use to beat her but there were no choice for her," and here she stopped.

I was focused on the story, as I was just looking at her face. The face clearly conveys her pain. Her tears were telling something, which I was unable to understand but I wanted to know whose story it was, and the answer kept me in shock for a minute as she answered, "The lady sitting in front of you is the girl in the story." Silence fell in the room. I could not control my emotions and myself. I hugged her and saluted her that in spite of being tortured for such a long period and being in the brothel, these women never demand anything.

She also told that her story is not unique. "There were hundreds of us, young girls from

Bangladesh, Nepal, and other parts of India sold into brothels."

"Why don't you try to escape from here?" I asked, and she said she once tried but failed, even though she cried, screamed for someone to help her, people just stood by watching, without even a look of sympathy.

"If even one man had tried to save me, my life would have changed. However, all of them stood there like mute spectators. Why does it happen that when any incident happens we act like an audience? Why do we not move forward to help?"

She finished by saying, "To the men who buy us, we are like meat. To everybody else in society, we simply do not exist." I was looking at her eyes; I have never seen so much of truth in anyone's eyes. Oh God, why do you make such cruel people on earth?

Her story and her words crushed my heart and make me ask myself a question: what are they made of? In spite of being so much tortured they didn't make any complain to the world.

I thank her and asked for leave but she stopped me and said "it's 4 o' clock, how you'll go," I said

"I'll manage," she said "no, leave at six" I said "What, you have any problem?" she said "no" and then she said "So you know everything about me, now tell me something about yourself, girlfriend and all."

"My name is Nasir, hailing from Allahabad and there is nothing interesting about me yet for those who want to know me; my entire being has universe in my heart, wound and pleasures. There are dreams in my eye, desires and curiosity. Know my soul and you will know me, and about a girlfriend, my answer is no." She laughed at me and called me a liar and the conversation continued. I was watching her smile, her *masti*, and was feeling bad for myself that at that time I was helpless to take her away out of this brothel.

"Don't you want to leave GB Road someday and find a good job?" I asked.

"Ma (the Didi, pimp) will never let me go, she is good to me and this is my home. Even if I'll leave this place where will I go? The society will always label me as prostitute. I am scared wherever I will be employed, the men will rape me. Even if I marry a prince tomorrow and wear expensive saris (dresses) and sit in a big car, people will still think

I am a prostitute. I cannot change that." My eyes remained glued to hers as she narrated her story.

I saw my wrist watch. It was 6 am, I asked her for leave and took out extra money to give her but she refused to take the amount and hugged me, wishing me all the best for my book.

I came out and started walking through the dark roads of GB Roads. During the time I was just thinking about her past and about all those women who have passed these stages. What amazing ladies? I feel like saluting them.

We have a fear of hell but these women have already seen hell before dying. We fight for our religion, but these women taught me a lesson that all religions are equal. Being literate we act illiterate, but being illiterate these women taught me so many things.

I came back to Ghaziabad where I rented a room. My next destination was Mumbai and Kolkata but for that I needed a handsome amount. I started following my daily schedule and started looking for a job to collect the amount for my next destination.

I started searching for a job on the internet, newspaper, etc. but did not find any job. One day

I went to Noida in search for a job and I came to know that in a BPO, a walk-in interview was going on. I went there for the interview and I got the job with a salary of 7000. I was satisfied because my father paid for my monthly expenses and the money I got as a salary I could collect and spend on my journey.

I got the shift of 3 pm to 12 pm, this continued for seven months, and after having a good amount I decided to leave the job to complete my journey. Therefore, one fine day, I left the job.

One night, a full moon was in the sky I was lying on bed and was thinking about these women's sadness and helplessness. How these women are working for pennies, to feed their families, to send their kids to good schools, renting their own body for their own food, forced to this profession, beaten, tortured.

Did we even know that the sex industry is one of the biggest and fastest growing criminal industries? (Approx. $100billion per year) and there are 20 million prostitutes, 42% of these are under 18 and 1.5 million child prostitutes in India? Traffickers inject steroids to young girls to make them look like adults, but in reality they are just teenagers. It has grown to eighteen times its size in the last 15 years.

At present there are more slaves than any other time in the world history. Saddening but the truth is that we are living in a "Slave World." No matter the slaves are from bonded labor, farms or flesh trade, all these forms of slavery put big question marks on our nation's integrity.

Mumbai (journey from Falkland Road to Congress house)

Arriving at at Mumbai felt like an assault on the senses. Thud, thud, thud, the coolies started pumping into the train even before it had come to a halt. They squeezed their way through the crowded door which was packed with passengers waiting to get off. I glared at a coolie who brushed past my chest but he had no time to even look at me. I cursed myself. I should've sat quietly on my seat till everybody else had got off.

Chatrapati Shivaji terminus was the last station; the train wasn't going to be running off anywhere. But no, I had to crowd into the passage with everybody pushing into each other like it was a local train.

#Area

I turned to avoid the strong smell of *chameli* that wafted from the hair of the woman standing in front of me.

"Don't push," I snapped at the man behind me who was digging his suitcase into the back of my legs.

Everybody was in a hurry, but in typical Mumbai fashion, nobody was getting anywhere. I looked at my watch once again. It was almost one hour since I had reached CST. Half an hour being squashed in the rush hour, this took me another half an hour to finally come out of the station.

The station from outside had such a beautiful look. After coming out of the station I was feeling hungry but didn't know what to eat and where to eat as I was very new in the city. While walking I saw Bada Pao, a famous thing to eat in Mumbai as much as I have heard and even at a very low cost. So I had Bada Pao and went ahead to find out a room for myself. Walking one kilometer away from the station just in front of the police choky on the other side of the road I found a person asking me whether I want a hotel. One thing was very different; he was continuously rubbing his nose when he asked me for the hotel. I said "Yes,

I want and at what price do you have?" And he said "rs 3000, a day," I said "Oh please, rs 3000? I don't want," but he says "With a room you'll get the girl also," I was bewildered, I just entered Mumbai and here itself it started. The man gave me a signal that it's not on a small level but on a big level. I said no to him and walked ahead to find out a room for myself. While walking I asked one person about the cheapest rooms and then I came to know about dormitory rooms. I walked towards the direction he told me for the dormitory. At the time I was walking on stairs, I saw some beautiful girls coming out from the small place which was connected with the hotel area. I was in doubt about these girls, from where this bulk of girls is coming out and who these girls were. I decided to find out later as I was very tired. I hired a bed to sleep.

In the evening, I came out to know about Kamathipura and its direction. As much as I know, the very simple thing to know about any place is to visit the local pan-wala, have something and you'll have the information you want. I followed the same procedure as I was looking for a pan-wala shop and on a little distance I found one. I saw a person sitting on a pillow with a big mustaches making pan by singing a song. I asked him for a pan, he said "Which type of pan you would love to have?" And with his dialect I guessed that he must hail from UP or Bihar. Taking the advantage of this, I said "The one which you like, but it should be full of love," he said "Are you from Bihar?" I said "No I am from UP," he laughed and asked, "So here for travelling?," I said "Yes, just came to see Kamathipura," he gave a smile and said "Just entered Mumbai and Kamathipura already?," I said "No, it's not that what you are thinking," then I narrated to him my story and asked him, "How can I visit Kamathipura, and what should be the safety tips?" then he told me, "Badii-e-bhidd bhadd wali jagah hai waise lal bazaar kay naam say famous hai par kamathis logo kay wajah say Kamathipura jana jata hai." He also told me that the area is divided into roughly fourteen lanes and divided according to regional and linguistic background of the sex workers.

He told me how to reach there through the local train. After having a conversation I went to find out about the incident that had happened to me earlier and for that I entered one bar named "Samundar bar" and when I entered, I was shocked by seeing the atmosphere. I was like, "Oh man; I have seen this in television only. Lots of beautiful girls standing, orchestra playing music, people drinking, talking with girls and wasting their money like water."

Seeing the environment, a question came to my mind about these girls, who are these girls? Are they also from the same category for which I am looking? I somehow got the idea but how to be sure about my answer so I went back to the same pan-wala bhaiya to know about these girls.

I asked him "Who are these girls?" Then he said "They all are students, some are house wives. Usually some work for glamour and some because of poverty."

Looking towards this entire situation, I came to the point that glamour and poverty are the two things which make them enter into all this and people take advantage of this.

I needed to visit Kamathipura so I decided to find more about this bar story later on. The very next day, I woke up and got ready for Kamathipura. I took the local train towards my destination. I need to board on a local bogie but I was new to this city and I didn't know about the first class as I boarded on that bogie only. Damn, bad start. Sometimes I feel how much bad luck I carry. I was asked to pay the penalty for sitting in first class as I was having a regular ticket. I told the TC that I am new here and the all the bogies look same then he says "there is a black line and a red and you have to board on the red one and you are on the black one." Man, what bad luck, but after lots of hard work I convinced him on rs 250 and finally got out of it.

Finally my destination, Grant Road station. After coming out of the station, I was heading towards one of the city's most menacing locales. I was not keen about the visit, in fact I am very skeptical, not because I am not well protected, but because the red light area is not the most fascinating place to be. When you see people of the same sex garishly displaying their bodies as if to be objectified only, a bag of mixed emotions surface. There is anger, there is sympathy, there is hatred or there is either absolute ignorance.

It is said that the red light just gets brighter post 9pm and business is at its peak.

I first passed by Falkland Road. The narrow pathway greets you with an unpleasant stench and you don't know from where it is coming. But the smell reeks of filthy sex, small money, poor women and hungry men.

The stench is augmented by the restaurants, which have their pantries outside. Sweaty men are cooking chicken tikkas and naan for the customers who want to have everything (both chicken and sex).

Falkland Road is also lined with three cinema halls of which I remember Roshan cinema.

On either side of the road, there are small buildings, each compartmentalized into small rooms. The doors of the ground floors are opened while the top floors have iron cages just like the one you find in elevators.

Girls in the red light would be dragged or molested by pushy men. At the time prostitution was at its peak, and men would literally line the doors for their turn. The cages were built on the ground and top floors to ensure that these girls remain within their safe havens and not loiter around in the "tolerated areas" and become victims of the crowd. These cages, though of not much use today, still stand rusted but strong in these partially dilapidated buildings. The women here are freely moving for their customers. They are approaching men, calling out to them, making sleazy gestures. Most are dressed in tight fitting clothes lining their stomachs which have developed a bubble with time. If they are wearing saris, you wouldn't be surprised if it doesn't cover the upper half of the body.

Plunging necklines, red lipstick and heavily powdered-these women are nothing close to being deceptive prostitutes. It is a mixed group of people from ages sixteen-sixty, from east (Bengal, Bangladesh, Assamese) north (Nepalese) and south (tamilians and kannadigas). You know they are commercial sex workers and they are having no reservations about it. They flaunt it, regardless of any condemnation. They are the cheapest of the lot (rs 50-500) and they have no qualms about it.

After Falkland Road I entered Forar Road, which is on the other side of Falkland Road, and I feel like I have approached a dead end. It is nothing like Falkland Road. Prostitution is close to redundancy here and cane workers and tall buildings line the road instead.

However, few meters ahead, the lanes of Kamathipura speak the same language of brothels.

Kamathipura is split into some fourteen lanes, each unique with its own story to tell. Some of these however bear the footprints of residential homes today, as several have now shifted base.

As I entered Kamathipura, one of the first things I noticed were the buildings. Since the history of Kamathipura dates back to early 1800's, it's not surprising to believe that buildings here are hundreds of years old. They are dilapidated, dirty and tightly packed together. From the narrow lane, it felt as if they were leaning into us, ready to swallow me.

As I continued on, I started to take notice of the people. There were men, young and old gathered in front of chai stalls. There were small children playing outside while their mothers prepared dinner on portable cooking stoves outside of makeshift one room huts. There were women walking by, carrying vegetables from the local market. If I had stumbled into this neighborhood, I would guess I was just in another poverty stricken section of Mumbai. But this is Kamathipura, a fourteen lane district, crowded with brothels and sex workers. Drugs and alcohol addiction prevails in this area and violence is the norm.

I learned a lot of horrifying details that day. Almost every building I passed was home to a brothel filled with young girls brought from villages and neighboring countries deceived by the ones they trusted most. They come with the promise of marriage, better lives and employment but instead are sold to brothel madams.

They are told they must buy back their freedom by renting brothel beds. They are told if they leave, their family will be hurt. Even worse, they are told that their families will never accept them back. In essence, they are brain washed.

While walking, I was thinking how easy it was to talk to a girl in Delhi and Allahabad, as somehow there was a fear in me after witnessing Kamathipura. I pray to Allah to help me and with faith in Allah I walked ahead. As it was already 8.30 pm, I decided to approach someone as soon as possible because I was afraid seeing that horrible environment.

So I started looking for a girl from whom I can hear the story and the hidden truth of her life.

I really didn't know that the girl whom I'll approach would be so practical, and that her strength will teach me such a lesson. While walking on a lane, I saw a woman, she must have been twenty-five-thirty years old, beautiful, short, less than five feet five inches and petite. A woman wearing a pink sari and blouse that wrapped around her like an Egyptian mummy. A black bindi, red bangles and flowing black curly hair, eyes looking for someone to whom she can talk and chit chat in spite of doing all that shit. Sparkling eyes and a large mouth that often finds the time to smile. There were flowers in her thick black hair. I walked towards her with lot of confidence and asked her for a full night because during this period she won't be in a hurry. First she looked at me fully and asked me to come in, but one thing I didn't know is why she laughed when she looked at me. Am I really so ugly or something else? Anyways I went inside with her into the room. It was small, clean, cool and intimate. It had a good ambience, probably reflecting the aura of the occupant. There are shadows lounging around and geckos are mating on the wall. While sitting in the room, I asked her name, she said "Nikita" and then she said she will comeback in two minutes. I said "Okay." While she was not in the room I was looking around her room which was having a chair, a small table with powder, lipstick and some makeup, a mirror, and pails of water under the cot.

A thin brown rope stretches from one end of the room to the other with some clothes hanging on it. There were her clothes, washed, wrung and left to dry.

After a minute, I heard Nikita saying, "Take the condom, your safety is my safety." I said "Condom – are you sure lady, I don't need it," then I passed a smile, she said "No no, nothing without a condom" I said "Okay, but you are taking me wrong, actually I am not here for sex," suddenly she replied, "If not for a sex, then for what are you here? People visit here for this only," then I told her everything about my book, my passion, to tell people about their pain, about their hidden truth, everything. She was listening very carefully and after ten minutes, she went away. She bought tea for me and said "I don't know if you are telling the truth or not but I don't know why I feel like I can trust you, so what do you want to know, ask," she poured me tea in a small stainless steel cup and we sat on her large bed and started our conversation.

The bed sheet was white and clean and the pillowcase was ugly green. She told me that she was married but her husband died in an accident years ago. She looked after two young children back home in her village in Assam from her earnings as a sex worker in Kamathipura. Her father was not working and in an accident her mother lost her eyes, so she is frail and blind and is still alive.

She doesn't want to talk about the details of growing up, hungry and homeless most of the time, under the scorching southern sun. Maybe she just doesn't want to remember the pain.

I saw scars on her body, knife wounds and burn marks. I asked her about that, and then she lifts her sari and shows me her arms and legs. I can see the knife and burn marks. Her body has withstood much unimaginable violence.

She talks about these injuries in a matter of fact voice as though reading out a child's report card. There was no drama, no tears, and no 'look at my sorry state' cries. Suddenly she says "How's the tea?" She asks, smiling, trying to cheer me up. Later she says, "I will cook for you," she says this happily, "That's if you feel like eating with me."

I was just looking at her face but was crying in my heart. But she was very brave. I said yes to the dinner.

The conversation continued, and she told me that she wants to live in this brothel till the last ebb of life. "I can't go anywhere now. This is my house. Whenever I want to leave, I leave for my village and send money every month for my life, my children's and for their education with the hope they will do well in life.

"There is nothing else in my life. I am a prostitute. It is my job. The lowest job ever. I am like the garbage can. Born to be used. I know we prostitutes are hated, disrespected and often made fun of. When you criticize a woman for her rotten character, you compare her with us." My eyes were just looking at her, as they did not want to move away from this woman. While having our conversation, she also asked about me. I introduced myself to her.

I was feeling very thirsty; she brought a glass of water for me. She told me that she is even booked for the weekends too. She keeps the tips and the gifts she gets. "I have customers I have known for years. I have loved too, but now I don't love like that. That mad, desperate love is over, thank God. My mind doesn't connect to the body. It's just a job. Many customers come and go; they talk and tell their problems. They pay me because I listen. No one listens to anyone in the big city. No one has time. Everyone has problems. When I hear them, I feel my problems are nothing. I am sure even you have problems. It's the human condition, we are meant to solve them. It's all our *karam*. After sometime we will leave this body and take new birth."

I was shocked to hear all this from her and ask her how she knows all this. She says "look at my life', is there any reason for all that happened? What have I done? Even I didn't have a chance to be a bad person. I was raped as a child. So there must be something I did in a previous life and this is my punishment." (Nikita was gang raped several times, had repeated abortions and several venereal diseases long before she turned eighteen and finally found deliverance in a brothel. Her family with the help of an agent sold her.) "When I will die, my punishment will be over and next birth will be good."

"You tell me. You are educated. If it is not my karam, why have I suffered like this?"

She told me that she was born Hindu and used to pray every morning. "I haven't studied much, but there has to be some natural power that makes us different from others. I pray just because what I feel is responsible for creating life. It makes me feel strong, secure and happy."

She brought more tea for me, as it was late night, or early morning I guess. The rooms were full. The cubicle's door is shut and there is noise intruding our space. Some girls, who have not been taken for the night, slept in the hall outside on charpoys laid on the ground.

While we were having tea she asked "Why don't you eat? It is not good to have so much tea. There is some rice and dal. I'll heat it. Let's eat," she insists. We eat together in clean, separate plates. She gave me a spoon so that I don't dirty my hands.

She giggled and talked like a school girl. She was kind and loving and wanted to pamper me.

"Do you miss your kids?" I asked. She said, "I am a mother, which mother won't? I am here for them only. One thing that happens good in my life was that God has given me two boys. So I am not worried. If they are girls anything can happen to them." She showed me the picture of both kids which was framed on the wall. Two little boys, short, thin, tanned, oiled hair, in matching black shirts with white stripes sitting astride a black motorcycle. "One is fourteen and the other one is nine years old. They do not know who their fathers are, but they definitely know who their mother is. I want to give them a proper education. When they will grow up, they will understand that bringing them up was not an easy task for me.

"Do you know that many of us treat our ill and aged parents with the money we earn? We send money, and the money is accepted. However, we are not allowed to visit our family members. How many of you know that we on a regularly donate money to various organizations who look after our slum children? Even you people do not know that why we are here. You know it is never our choice."

She loved Hindi films and saw at least one a day and she loved even Hollywood but the ones dubbed in Hindi. She liked action and romance and even the scary flicks.

I asked her about her daily schedule. She said, "I wake up late, but it depends on customer traffic.

If the traffic is heavy the brothel gets a life at noon."

She also told that customers can stay in the brothel for weeks on end. Customers can stay as long as they want if they can pay.

Madam (a lady who was a former sex worker in the same brothel) wakes up early every day and looks into the provisions and other details. Biryani, tandoor dishes and kebabs can be ordered from nearby restaurants. Girls do not entertain customers during their menstrual cycle but hang around and chat. It's holiday time then. They also eat out with customers.

Nikita joked and laughed till tears trickled from her eyes. I wanted to salute this woman and her braveness. I simply can't fathom her and the others in the brothel.

We face lots of problems, but during difficult times our nature changes, we get aggressive, and many more, but I don't understand how Nikita and others keep laughing at life when it has always mocked them. Truly, we should learn the lesson from these ladies in spite of cursing them because their torture and their problems are very big as compared to us.

Finally I had a last tea with her, hugged her and said a lovely good bye. But before saying good bye, I promised her that one day I will tell the world about her and about her people, their pain, their lifestyle, their painful smile, everything.

After coming out of the brothel, I started walking towards the auto stand for Grant Road railway station. While walking on the lane, I was looking at those women and I was really feeling very bad, I asked my soul how these women keep laughing in life, when it has always mocked them.

Life dances and you have to dance with it. Each moment is afresh moment in the dance, and you have to be present for it.

Slavery is defined as a civil relationship whereby one person has absolute power over another and controls his life, liberty and fortune. On this day, I saw slavery at its core.

I called for a taxi and asked him to leave me at Grant Road railway station. He told me the fare according to the meter and I boarded. While sitting, I was only thinking about Nikita and yet was unable to scratch out the images of burn and knife wounds on Nikita's body. Her dazzling eyes, the wisdom of her words and the smile that roped in all the joys of the world in its loving expanse, in a badly lit cubicle of a brothel on the first floor of a building steadily falling apart in one of the most notorious flesh districts in the world.

I was about to reach the station but I don't know why I asked him to stop the auto and told him to take me back to the same place from where he picked me up.

He asked "Are you sure sir?" I said "Yes I am, and do me a favor, take me to the chocolate shop from where I can get a chocolate."

After picking up the chocolate, he dropped me back at Kamathipura. I came out from the auto and went straight to the place where I met Nikita. When I reached the place, I found that Nikita was not there; my eyes were looking for her. I don't know why. But it was all without a reason. On a side corner of the wall, my eyes saw the girl that they were looking for. I slowly and quietly went there and howled on her ears, she got shocked and it brought a smile to her face and then I asked her, "Can I have one more last tea with you?" she smiled and said "Yes." She asked me why I am back. I said I don't know why but my heart said to come back so I came back. She suddenly hugged me tightly. I can easily see the tears in her eyes but hats off, how brave they are, always presenting themselves as they are very brave... We had tea, and then I gave her a chocolate and said a final bye with a promise to see her soon. Before I was leaving, Nikita said, something that really made me feel sad. She said, "When you write about us, do write that we do not need sympathy from those people who know nothing about our struggle. That would only make them great, and us, heinous creatures." Each word she spoke felt as if we all were being slapped hard.

I do not know why I came back but I did what my heart says to do. After meeting her, I moved forward towards the Congress house. I decided to visit this place on the same day because I hardly have enough days left.

Before I begin, let me give you a briefer. The Congress house is located in one of the by lanes of lamington road near the Grant Road police station.

Once a beehive of India's freedom fighters, the Congress house that is an enclave of seven buildings is literally all surrounded by a mujra complex.

It's only sightings with history are the names of the building like Sarojini Sadan, Dadabhai Manzil, Jinnah Hall, Congress restaurant and beer bar.

In 1972, our Prime Minister of India, Mrs. Indira Gandhi had setup a sangeet academy at the Congress house. The academy was home to members of the Agra community of singers and dancers who organized dance shows for the royals over 300 years ago.

She must have not realized what it was going to be happening today. The Congress house were fond of song and dance. So after their day's work, a mujra session would usually be called for late in the night and woman would sing and dance to the tunes of tablas and harmoniums. This is how the place went on to become a mujra complex and also flourished with time.

The atmosphere of a mujra's performance is usually unique in itself. Mirrored walls, huge chandeliers and brightly lit rooms that are filled with drinkers. These men shower notes on the girls or gift them with garlands of notes.

I attended one and it was less like a typical mujra and more like a dance bar-this one is at the Congress house. The entrance has an old board which reads "sangeet academy." As I entered, I saw a group of male members and female members. People stare from floors above and are suspicious about the irregulars around.

However, I must say, unlike Kamathipura and Falkland Road, the girls are extremely beautiful. (I don't know why these beautiful girls are slaves in their own minds. Are they convinced that there is no hope for them? There is no life outside of the hell they live in. There is no one that will accept them for who they are, don't know why.)

Lustrous black hair, milk-like skin and designer or expensive saris. Yes, this not exactly the red light area, this was the place where mujras or kothas take place. The girls comes from Agra, UP, and Delhi.

I attended one of the mujras sessions; the feel of the original mujras devastatingly tweaked. There were mirrors, tabla players, a singer and bling bling lights. All apart from the musicians are stationary, they just sit and watch.

Incidentally, they do not work as prostitutes but nachne wallis instead. If they sleep, it is for the master who feeds them enough so that they do not shift loyalties.

I moved out in ten minutes. Well, this is some slice. One dark, one light, one monetarily exhausting and the other financially tempting. This is a slice of "red light" Mumbai.

I came out and decided to leave for the hotel as for the day I was done. I took the auto for the hotel. I had a dinner outside and after having dinner, I went on the terrace. I was sitting and was looking towards this city, city known for its glamour and was just memorizing my past journey and was thinking about those women whom I met. Seriously, what lives they live, I mean from early age until the end, only pain but still they never show it to anyone. The question of Sweta lingered in my mind, was she born a prostitute? The burns of Nikita was not letting me sleep.

I was helpless, I cannot do anything for them but that very day I decided that one day I'd definitely do something for them.

I do not understand that why rich people waste their money for such stupid things or even on hiring beautiful girls for their lust. Why people waste thousands and thousands of rupees like water in a dance bar but nobody even tries to give them work or tries to free them from that jungle.

I don't say it to stop prostitution but the ones who want to be in this, let them, and the ones who don't, please let them free, at least give them some work and I believe that result will be higher than the expectation.

Today we fight for everything, demand our rights, protest to fulfill our demand, but these women after facing so much of pain and torture never come to protest or demand.

"Tiring Tiring" alarms ringing continuously and that sound irritates me so much that I switch it off and slept again. My God, when my eyes open it was 7.45, damn, forty-five minutes for the train to depart. I thought I would miss the train. With my full energy, I got ready quickly and ran towards the station. I even forgot to brush. When I reached the station, I saw the engine blowing its whistle, damn what bad luck. Trains are usually late but today this one was on time.

I ran towards the train as fast as I can and jumped into my bogie. Deep breath, finally in the train. I satisfied myself that, yes Nasir, you are in the train. After a moment, I proceeded towards my seat to settle my luggage. It was the upper berth, I believe. I was happy because I will not be disturbed by anyone. I kept my luggage, had a brunch and went to sleep again.

After having a long stay in Mumbai, I was heading towards my next destination "Kolkata." Viewing the pictures of Meerganj(Allahabad), GB Road(New Delhi), Kamathipura(Mumbai) I was accepting the different picture of Sonagachi because before visiting all these places I was expecting the same environment of all the places but my journey changed my whole thought. Every area had its own story.

After visiting these areas, I came to know many things about these women, which many of us really do not know. We just see them as commercial sex workers, but we never try to feel their pain or try to help them out. My feelings were totally attached to them and the respect for them was on a different level.

I do not know why we curse them, why we do not give them equality, why we write bad comments or sexual comments using the word whore, Randi, Vishay on social networking sites. I really feel bad when I see those types of comments on social media.

Why does everyone from the outside world only care about condom awareness and STI checks? Why don't they ever ask how they are or whether they want anything else in life?

Why are these women treated like slaves? Is it just because they share their bed with many people or it is just because their lifestyle is different from us? On the other hand, is it just we call them whore, or that they are whores?

Have we ever thought how safe our sisters, wives, daughters, mothers are? Have we? No, we have not and why? Because these women are whores and their work is to exchange sex with money, that is all we want to think. However, have we ever imagined a situation where if these women don't exist, then what will happen? Imagine the number of people who are visiting these women on a daily basis for pleasure and if they did not find them, then?

I once saw a dog that was very hungry as if he had not have food for one full day and he was looking for food everywhere but he failed to find any food. After roaming here and there he found shit, and he ate that, and this taught me a lesson that if we are hungry or the level of hunger is unbearable, then we'll eat whatever we'll get.

Now imagine if a person fails to get these women then he will be like the same dog that will attack anyone to bring down his level of hunger. Then will it be possible for our daughters, sisters, wives, mothers to walk safely on the street? No, they will not.

We do not even know that how much of a favor they are doing for us by sharing their bed without their willingness. Who loves to do this work? But what we give them is disrespect, abuse, an inequality and more. Have we ever asked ourselves if they were born prostitutes? Do they like to work in this brothel? No, we have never. They must be someone's sister, daughter, wife and a mother but what happened to them? Some evil people just for their sake kidnap them, sell them, and force them to enter into this brothel.

It's really easy to point our fingers at anyone but imagine if this happens with us, touchwood, I pray that it never happens but if not us then someone else. Then is it the fault of that girl, who only became the victim and her whole life is spoiled? But we are not ready to see all this. We just know that if she is a prostitute then she is spoiling our city, our society, and our culture.

Kolkata (a dark night in Sonagachi)

A popular city in India known for its culture and tradition. I looked up at the night sky, which showed a stunning display of orange and red colors. Birds were cheerfully warbling as I checked my wrist watch. It was 8 pm. I walked through the eerie dark roads of Kolkata. I was heading for Sonagachi, the prostitute-clogged red light district of Kolkata.

"Sonagachi" the largest red light area of Asia, a place known for many wrong reasons, said to shelter over 30000 sex workers.

The area came to be known as Sonagachi from a Sufi saint Sona Ghazi whose tomb (mazar) is located in the locality. He would not have ever imagined in his wildest dreams that he will become famous for such things one day!

A Night that gets brighter after 9 pm and business is at its peak.

When will this era of women slavery end?

Mostly Nepalese, Bangladeshis, and Rajasthani prostitutes have dominated this area, which accounts for the total estimated population of sex workers in this area to be 10000.

The sex workers in this area consider themselves as a thing just to entertain men, ad this is how they earn their bread and butter. Few of them have joined this profession by choices whereas a few have been dumped in this industry forcefully or because of betrayal. In addition, few among them been brought into this flesh trade by illegal means.

The workers here long every minute to lead a normal life like any other person does. However, unfortunately they have been forsaken by good fortune and hence, leading such lives with no hopes at all left for their betterment.

As I tread through the red light district, I observed multistoried buildings where women glanced out from their balconies. I observed a dapper man conversing with a sex worker. I came across many young jaunty young students who were dawdling around doing nothing. I could see many semi-clad girls usually in their early twenties standing outside their apartments luring their customers.

As I aimlessly wandered around the red light district of north Kolkata, someone tapped my back from behind. I looked behind and I found a woman around 45 years old.

"Are you new to this place?" she asked.

"Yes, I am,"

"Where are you from?" she asked.

"Allahabad," I cleared my throat and continued, "Why are you asking all this?"

"Want to see a beautiful side of this dark place?" she sheepishly smiled at me.

I was amazed at the way she impressed me.

She was old, but she looked gorgeous. She had her beauty intact.

She asked me to follow her to the apartment. "Namaskar Didi..." a few girls said as we were walking. A few of those girls smiled at me as I followed her. She was trying to befriend me but my intentions were clear enough the moment I entered the red light district.

As I entered the apartment, I saw the faded paint on the walls. I could smell the dirty odor of semen as I climbed up the stairs.

After a minute, she gave me a room number and said, "A beautiful girl is waiting for me inside the room. Trust me you would love her," she added.

Sex is something, which gives them bread and butter to these girls. Over thousands of men visit the place every day to fulfill their desire. Life is like a jigsaw puzzle. Strange things keep happening around and we just cannot find ways to get rid of it. It is a vicious circle.

I headed for the room she indicated. I knocked on the door. A beautiful girl with a slim body wearing a sari opened the door. She greeted me and invited me in. I entered the room and sat on the bed. She went to close the door and sat next to me. She was wearing a black sari. My God, my favorite color and in that, she was looking so beautiful. Moreover, this beauty is being destroyed every day.

She unhooked her blouse as I helplessly observed her. "Can I ask you for a favor?" She asked. "Yes, what can I do for you?" "While having sex, please do it slowly as it will hurt me," and then she completely undressed herself. I witnessed innocence as she spoke.

"What's your name?" I asked her.

"Anjali," she said.

As she was sitting next to me, I was admiring her beauty and at the same time, I cursed her plight. She was the same height as me with a slim body. Her hair was neatly braided. She had a long face with milky smooth skin. Her eyes were so mysterious and deep, that one could actually be lost in the bright day light. Her eyelashes hid the eternal universe behind. Her nose was tiny but was looking cute. Her lips were as red as the blood of martyrs.

I looked at her rosy cheeks and the dark mole beneath her lips, which adorned her beauty. I seemed to have been lost in her beauty. She lay completely naked facing me. I looked straight into her eyes, which attracted me and spoke of innocence. My heart could not accept her in this state. I ask her to dress herself but she covered her bare body with the blanket. How could a woman like her indulge in such activities? A beauty that is broken by the street dogs every day. This perturbed me.

What a beautiful girl! I never expected to see such beauty in my whole journey and never expected to get a girl like this in this jungle.

"You are a handsome boy and you are that pearl in the ocean which every girl would die for," she asserted.

"Aahh… Thanks Anjali but I take it as a compliment." She came closer to me and tried to kiss me and I was very seduced. "You certainly know how to seduce a man," I said.

"Unfortunately, that is what I have been doing all these days to different men. Doing something against my wish, fantasies and fortune," These words of her cracked me into pieces. "What happened?" I questioned her.

"I am not destined to be here. I have fantasies that will not materialize," she replied.

"I have been trying to chase my fantasies, fantasies which hold my fortune but I could only have fantasies of," I said.

"You are not right. Fantasies and fortune are not parallel paths. Fortune embodies our fantasies. It is just that we need to work on them by our actions. But, I got no right to talk about all this while I am in this filth," she added.

"If only fantasies come true, I would have been a famous personality in India. Sometimes

I feel like a bird whose wings are cropped which prevent me to fly high." She continued.

She was speaking and I was just listening and every word she spoke, she touched my heart to some extent. I had fallen for her eyes. Her eyes turned moist and filled with tears.

"I am a trash bin where men come to dump their sorrows and seek pleasure," she cried. There was a complete silence for a moment.

"How did you land in this place?" I asked her.

"Only a woman who is born mad or insane would love to be here. Unfortunately, I was born and sold into this brothel. My mother was very beautiful but poverty has covered us. Everything was going good but she was caught in this mysterious world of sex when she was young. Many men knocked on her door to quench their thirst. She pleased them and she became pregnant. I was born. I failed to know my father for my mother slept with many men and for me she was mother and father. Days and days pass, I started earning money by dancing in between the cars on the busy road.

"As time passes, my pitiful earning from dancing was not enough to feed my family and

I became one of the hundreds of thousands of children sold into sexual slavery.

"Drugged and confused, violently raped several times, but I blindly accept my fate. I was beaten until I accepted to get sexual with a man of three times of my age. I became the victim of sexual crime many times each night. I even tried to escape, but I was beaten or worse. This is my future until I die.

"I was often asked if given a chance, I would go back or not. However, my answer was always NO. You know why? Because your society has failed to give us education, family, livelihood. All you people did was act as a moral police at times.

"I sell my body, and I got enough guts to admit that. I don't steal. I am not dishonest. I sell what belongs to me, is solely mine. I don't beg for money." My eyes remained glued to hers as she narrated her story. She wore her blouse and draped her black sari.

After all this, finally I told her the reason why I am here in Sonagachi.

"I don't regret coming here. Your eyes enclose the mysteries that hurt me. It hurts to see a beautiful flower in a puddle of mud. I did not expect that I will meet a girl like you over here. You don't deserve to be here," I said.

"Thank you Nasir for your kind words but now I am habitual of all this and it doesn't hurt me. I am used to it. And of course you haven't done anything for the money you have spent on me," she gave a smile. I smile back at her when she said that.

If I tell the truth, I was fallen for her. Beautiful girl, full of innocence at the time. I could feel an urge to take her with me but I was unable to take her out.

"One last question if you do not mind. I have heard the nongovernmental organizations (NGOs) work on prevention of HIV and AIDS among sex workers in Sonagachi. Are you aware of this?"

"There are many NGOs here in Sonagachi. On a regular basis, they organize shows, events on HIV and AIDS and sex workers rights. We were also taught to insist on the clients to wear a condom, which is important to be safe from the killer disease (HIV and AIDS). They also set up a testing camp for that. Even if we insist on condoms, customers pay an extra 25 percent as a bribe to the aunty. We are not allowed to go to the camps."

"Thanks for the night Anjali," I said. She smiled and said, "I hope that we will meet again soon."

She bid a good bye as I left. I was looking at her, as I knew how I was feeling when I was leaving her. God, why did you make such bad people who spoil the life of others?

Anjali's life, her beauty, her intelligence, her future, and her hope been stolen. It is more than bleak. I left my heart with her but I was happy that I met a girl who believes that Prostitution Not Always a Choice but poverty and situation make it a choice. There are many Shaguftas, Swetas, Nikitas, and Anjalis who are caught in this mysterious web of sex world, but we can never comprehend the pain in their heart. It's impossible to imagine the situation these women and children are in.

"People tend to be put off by the idea of selling sex,

But if you spend a winter's night with one of them

And talk her about her family and so on,

You're likely to find she's just like any other woman"

— EIJI YOSHIKAWA

Damn, it's everywhere. No part of the country is spared from this crime. Moreover, women are becoming the victim of this slavery.

After meeting Anjali, I walked on the streets of Sonagachi and I met one more girl standing out wearing a yellow sari with a big circle red bindi and curly hair. I asked her if I could have five minutes to talk. Earlier she was ignoring, but when I briefed her about my journey, she said yes to give her five minutes and to answer my questions.

So can you tell me how you reached Sonagachi at this very age?

I was ten years when I came to Sonagachi and I hail from Nepal. I am Hindu and I tell this to every customer when they ask and my name is Kiran. I have no family. Ma (pimp) is my family. She looks after me, she feeds me, she even gave me a sari for Durga Puja but in return she wants business and I have to work. When I was little, one man came and said he will keep me with him and he will marry me with a good person, and one fine day, he brought me to Kolkata and left me here at one of the dirtiest brothels.

What's your present age?

I am fifteen years old but I tell people that I am twenty years old.

How many and what kind of customers visit in a day and how does the business work?

If I talk about the brothel then there are twenty to twenty-five girls in eight rooms. Not every girl works for Didi. Some come to chitchat as at this time business is slow. Some girls have hired a room on a rent of rs 5000 a month. My earlier rate was 1000 to 1500 and those high category girls charge 5000 to 6500, but now we work on a fixed rate system, all for rs 500 per client for one hour. 50% of the money earned from each customer goes to Didi. Customer has to pay 25% extra to her as a service charge.

Now the clients are mainly college boys, lawyers, married men, foreigners, taxi drivers and restaurant owners.

Sometimes police raid the brothel but Didi slips them some money and offers her best girl to them and the business resumes.

Don't you want to leave this place? Don't you want to live like others?

Who wants to live here? But Didi will not let me go. I never want to be here but nobody comes for my help. Everyone just come to take pleasure in my body and when finished with their work, they leave. That is what I am! A trash bin where people come to throw their dirt. The tag that I have of a prostitute will never let me live anywhere because where ever I go, people will always think I am a prostitute. I cannot change that.

Do you know that these traffickers everyday get five to ten girls as young as sevenyears old. Every four minutes, one girl is kidnapped. I do not know when we will start thinking about them. Making NGOs and letting them function is not a big deal. The government has to do something and I am waiting for that day when these leaders will look on the serious matter of these women, leaving behind the vote bank politics.

Reason for Entry

It is found that majority of these women in India work as prostitutes due to lacking resources to support themselves or their children. Most do not choose this profession but out of necessity, often after the breakup of a marriage or after being disowned and thrown out of their homes by their families. The children of these women are much more likely to get involved in this kind of work as well.

As during my whole journey towards all these brothels, I interview a random sample of 130 women in Allahabad and all the metropolitan areas. Of those, sixteen women claimed that they had come of their own accord, whereas the remaining 110 women claimed to have been introduced into the sex trade by agents. 84% had been raped which makes me wonder how they could stay in this profession if it causes them so much pain.

- ➤ Neighbor in convenience with parents = **09**
- ➤ Neighbor as pimps = **15**
- ➤ Aged sex workers from same village or locality = **23**
- ➤ Unknown person/ accidental meeting with pimp = **22**
- ➤ Husband (not legally married) = **02**
- ➤ Husband (legally married) = **01**
- ➤ Mother/sister/near relative in this profession = **15**
- ➤ Lover giving false hope of marriage or job and selling to brothels = **15**
- ➤ Close acquaintance false hope of marriage = **12**

Conclusion

After visiting Kolkata and all the metropolitan cities, my journey ends. A long journey from Allahabad to Kolkata, from which I came to know many truths running beneath the surface. Every place has its own story. Every woman has her past, which is full of pain and torture. Nobody wants to work in this profession but poverty makes them do it and people take advantage of this.

Tell me one thing: if these women are prostitutes than what is wrong in that? If they will not do this then how they will afford their bread and butter for their children? We as a society are not ready to help them. Once a girl is kidnapped and sold out into the brothel, at an age when she doesn't even know what is good or bad for her, who in her whole life has only seen slavery, what will she do? Only left with a choice of selling her body because we don't want to help them, and the government is busy with other issues.

We can do only one thing that can be easily done, we can make fun of them, try to keep them away from us, exclude them from society and at last, abuse them, hurt them etc.

If a person faces so much inequality, then I believe that these women are not wrong. Today we talk of equality, but where is equality? I cannot see. Can't we change this, which has been running for years and years? Why can't we give them equality and respect, and help them to come out of this?

During my whole journey, whenever I think of these women, one quote of Victor Hugo always reminded me of one thing, that "slavery" still exists.

We say that slavery has vanished from European civilization,

But this is not true.

Slavery still exists, but now it applies only to women

And its name is Prostitution.

(Victor Hugo)

I know I am one among those writers who have written books on the same topic but I do not want that after reading my book, people keep it aside. I want a change. I want people to bring change in their thoughts and at least give them respect and equality in society, because it is impossible to feel the pain and comprehend the situation that these women and children are in. They were not born prostitutes, they were among us. Born into a respected family but due to poverty and some evil people, they lost everything. Every single girl has a dream, intelligence, sees the future like us, but everything has been stolen from them.

Is it their fault? They do not even know how to make a choice, what is good or bad at the time when they were kidnapped or sold into these dirty brothels.

People visit these red light areas to do research, make films, and the media visits for stories, the police goes to raid brothels, but nobody visits them to actually ask these ladies what they want or just spend time with them. We often hear talk of women empowerment, of human rights, women's safety. If it is so then why are GB Road, Kamathipura and many more running freely?

Everybody knows about these places but nobody is doing anything about it. Sometimes I just think, what is our society doing? These women are a part of our society too.

Why are governments not doing anything to stop prostitution? I guess poor lives cost less than pennies! Moreover, I believe if this will stop, then how will the government make the world's richest person lose their pocket?

I know I am against the legalization and I know people will say that if prostitution stops, then rape will increase, but I believe that today, having prostitution alive, we are still having rape cases at a very high rate, even cases which have never been highlighted.

How much longer will women face torture, sexual abuse, harassment etc.? It's time to bring change. I am against legalization because I want this sex slavery to stop completely. We don't even imagine the trauma and exploitation of prostitutes and if it is legal, then it will lead to increase in trafficking of young girls into the flesh trade and work as an open market of sex trading.

I hear many people saying that it is their work or profession. Is it a profession? I am sorry, my friend, but I don't believe that, because it's a crime committed against humanity.

I don't understand one thing, people behind closed doors are doing hanky-panky with young girls, housewives, college students but nobody points them out because they are white collar people, however it is very difficult to delimitate such a right, so what should be considered as prostitution? If a female provides a male with sex before marriage, then having sex before marriage called as prostitution?

According to me, today pornography also plays the role in increasing the demand of sex. It is destroying our new generation because today during our time we never knew how a baby is born. We were always told that an angel comes and puts a child near the mother, but today even a seventh standard boy knows everything about sex and how a baby is born. How?

Pornography; it is ruling our children's minds. My dear parents, my reason to write about this point is very clear because I know as parents we want to provide everything to our children but we don't know which track they are moving on. In my journey, I found a large number of school youngsters dawdling here and there in every brothel. How? Who told them?

I would also love to request parents to keep in contact with your daughters today because today glamour is killing our generation. We as parents give them whatever is there in our hands but sometimes, it is impossible to fulfill every demand of our children and this takes our children down the wrong path.

Today many young college students, boys as well as girls, away from their homes are being trapped in this world of glamour, which looks very beautiful, but they don't know they are entering into a jungle where there are many options to enter but no exit. A person offers them good money, shows them glamour but never tells them that they are entering a jungle that has no exit. More than 90% women in this jungle expressed a desire to leave but they need help.

We have one central government and particular state governments but still no one is bothered about them. I believe the sex and drugs industry cost more than a poor life.

During my whole journey, the places I visited and the women whom I met really need help.

We die once but they are dying daily with every different person. I wonder how these women are surviving. If I ask anyone of us to be there for a whole day, trust me, you will want to kill yourself. However, hats off to them, what brave ladies! Today through my book, I want to ask you people –

- ➢ **Why are these women treated like slaves?**

- ➢ **Why don't they get the chance to be what they want?**

- ➢ **Why are these kids exposed to things they should not know?**

- ➢ **Why are we as a society forced to accept this?**

- ➢ **How much longer will the slavery of women continue?**

    Get up stand up:

    Stand up for their rights!

    Awake Arise!

    Help them...

My aim is to free them from this jungle where slavery exists and I hope that they never to go back to this jungle again. I trust myself and had faith in Allah that one day you and I will relocate all the girls from these brothels. I know I am talking about something that is impossible, but impossible itself says I M POSSIBLE.

I believe everyone deserves life with dignity and a good future, without selling flesh as written in article 21 of the constitution.

It is impossible to feel their pain and to imagine the situation that these women and their children face. But if we truly come up to help them, teach them, truly help them to come out of this heinous trade and give them some decent work, then I believe we can give them a choice that,

"Prostitution, Not Always a Choice"

www.ingramcontent.com/pod-product-compliance
Lightning Source LLC
Chambersburg PA
CBHW031407250726
48656CB00002B/575